A STUDIO OF ONE'S OWN

ANN STOKES

A STUDIO OF ONE'S OWN

ANN STOKES

the NAIAD PRESS inc.

°1985°

Printed in the United States of America

First edition

The last fifteen lines of "My Name Is Judith . . ."
by Judy Grahn are reprinted with permission,
Copyright © 1978, from a sequence called "Con-
frontations with the Devil in the Form of Love"
in THE WORK OF A COMMON WOMAN.
Originally published by Diana Press, then re-
issued by St. Martin's Press and finally by
Crossing Press.

Cover and title page as well as book design by Pat Hill
Edited by Dolores Klaich
Glossary illustration by Ann Goldsmith
Typeset by Sandi Stancil

Library of Congress Cataloging in Publication Data

Stokes, Ann.
    A Studio of one's own.

    1. Artists' studios—New Hampshire.   2. Women
artists—New Hampshire—Biography.   3. Lesbians—
New Hampshire—Biography.   I. Title.
NX510.N38S7   1985   700'.92'2 [B]   85-258
ISBN 0-930044-64-9

. . . not until we have ground we can call our own
to stand on
& weapons of our own in hand
& some kind of friends around us
will anyone ever call our name Love,
& then when we do we will all call ourselves
grand, muscley names:
the Protection of Love,
the Provision of Love & the
Power of Love.

. . . Judy Grahn

CONTENTS

August 14, 1933. Mother and author.

Prologue

Ann Stokes: In the summer after I graduated from high school, my mother and father pushed me into an American Friends Service Committee workcamp. Every morning we twenty emotionally gangly, naive, and highspirited souls gathered in Quaker silence for twenty minutes, ate breakfast, and went to our major job of building forms and pouring concrete. We cooked meals, lived simply, and grew muscles enough to build and complete a ford across a small river, thus enabling the rural population to drive through spring flooding for the necessities of life.

One of us was a pianist and sculptor — my first encounter with an artist, my first friendship with someone who knew the worth of feelings. An internal and global search rampaged through her. She asked/

talked/listened. Her propulsion to make sense of con-
fusion forced me to take beginning cognizance of my
own psyche; from my desert a small spring erupted.
I had no idea how complicated, how despairing, how
full of richness it all would be. Her moods were re-
flected on her face — when affirmed, she looked beautiful; when upset, just awful.

All of us came to life that summer, but it was she
who reached my heart. I remember her on her lower
bunk, her feet nudging me where I lay on the upper
one, sending me out of the cabin at midnight riddled
with laughter, only to calm down on the two-holer.
One afternoon our concave, pinch-nezed counselor
took me aside and with ominous overtones said,
"You really like Catherine a lot, don't you?" It was
then that I knew, in a hare's breath, I was in love
with a woman.

In the thirty years since, all I came to value at
that Quaker camp has expanded, both gradually and
in great rushes. I live in the country now. Special smells
rise from the pine needles when the sun hits them hot
in summer. The shapes of the tall pines show grand
changes from original directions. Six large ashes spotted
at random have limbs as big as most of their neighbors'
trunks. A low-lying rock became a prehistoric lizard
through my lover's eyes and remains so through mine;
under the snow that hibernated her this winter, her
flanks took a peaceful curve; she slept an ancient sleep.

Some woods-walks are for seeing, some for smelling,
some for thinking, some suddenly exclaim the first
breath of a poem. On some, I spew anger at the ignorant

destruction of what makes invisible, and visible, life tick. Others make me revel in the visible and invisible women who make one's blood pick up a pulse. Oh women women women! How we bring forth for each other all that has lain dormant. We rise to take action against the Pentagon, travel to Nicaragua for peace, stand at trials of rape, write of our own destructiveness from the basements of our psyches so that the horror may be transformed in the light of day. We change at the sight of purple, partake in a centuries-spanning Dinner Party, see with clarity our common woman strength, move into the political spotlight, climb the ladder to sinister wisdom.

Returning to the silence of Quaker worship, my soul renews. I see painting, singing, dancing as a path toward peace; our minds and bodies stretch to their utmost, and diminish destruction to a small dead twig.

~ ~ ~ ~ ~

On Easter Sunday, 1977, three dear lezzie-fairs came to my home in the woods of New Hampshire. Over dinner, a question came forth from fantasies, dreams, possibilities: "What do you think of building a studio for women artists?"

West Chesterfield, N.H.
1984

Dolores Klaich: I remember saying to Ann, "Be sure to keep a journal. It'll be part of our history "

As it happened, my life took a turn after that 1977 Easter planning session for the women's studio, and I did not visit Ann at her home on Welcome Hill again until six years later, the summer of 1983.

That summer I was traveling in New England, gathering research for a book about contemporary lesbianism, and I knew that I wanted to touch base with Ann Stokes. I had heard that the Studio had been built and already had housed a number of women artists. But I had forgotten that I had been in on the original idea, indeed had walked the woods that long-ago Easter to find the site.

When I arrived at Ann's 112-acre, heavily wooded mountaintop, with its breathtaking due-west view of Vermont, I found the same strong, funny, principled woman I had known in the mid-70s, the no-nonsense, Quaker-bred social activist who is one of the best laughers I have ever met. We compared greying heads and were pleased.

After dinner, I started our interview and when we came to talk of the Studio (which, because I had arrived after dark, I had not yet seen), Ann said, "You, Klaich, were part of that idea." It all came back to me — the weekend, the excitement of Ann's announcement of her plan, walking the woods to look for a site . . . I asked, hoping, "And did you keep a journal?" "Yup," said Ann.

The next morning, sitting on Ann's deck in glorious sun, drinking a cup of her famous strong coffee, I opened the journal. It was housed in an artist's sketch-book, 11" × 8½", was full of photographs, and contained not only Ann's musings, but the words of other women. In different colored inks and pencils, it chronicled the building of the Studio. Excited, I thought: A logbook. Undeniable history. I must show this to Barbara Grier.

Part I of what you are about to read is that logbook.

East Hampton, N.Y.
1984

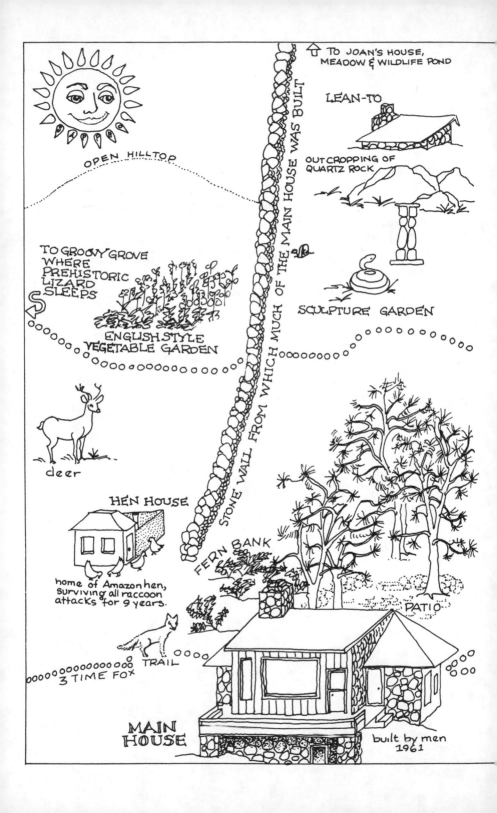

OPEN HILLTOP

TO JOAN'S HOUSE,
MEADOW & WILDLIFE POND

LEAN-TO

OUTCROPPING OF
QUARTZ ROCK

TO GROOVY GROVE
WHERE
PREHISTORIC
LIZARD
SLEEPS

S

ENGLISH STYLE
VEGETABLE GARDEN

SCULPTURE GARDEN

STONE WALL FROM WHICH MUCH OF THE MAIN HOUSE WAS BUILT

deer

HEN HOUSE

home of Amazon hen,
surviving all raccoon
attacks for 9 years.

FERN BANK

PATIO

3 TIME FOX   TRAIL

MAIN
HOUSE

built by men
1961

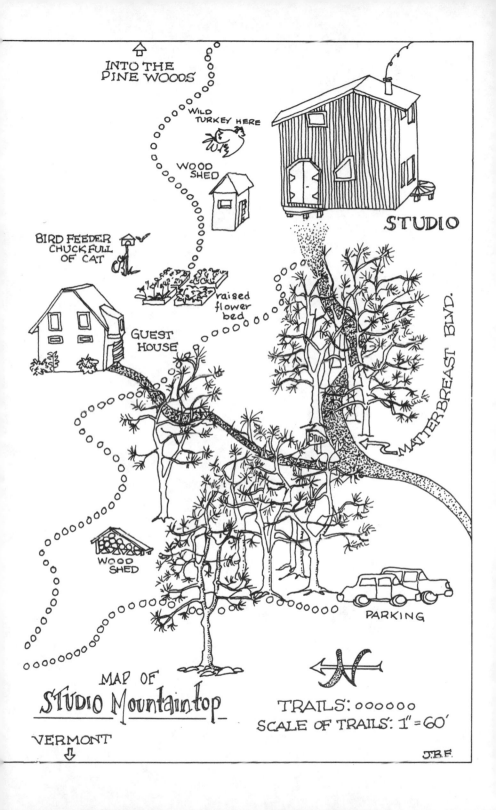

PART I

THE BUILDING
OF THE STUDIO

The Core Builders:

Ann Goldsmith
Doris (Tai) Hazard
Pat Hill
Seashell
Ann Stokes

Ann Stokes: April, 1977 ... I have often thought of willing my New Hampshire home and land to MacDowell, as an adjunct to their artists' colony in Peterborough. But as I receive their mail and contemplate those New York dinners to raise a million, I realize I want to stay away from institutions. What I want to have and to give to women is an informal atmosphere in a semi-rustic way of life, a combination of civilized and do-it-yourself, so that too much time isn't taken up with stoking the wood stove or writing by candlelight. To save money and to live a bit more country, there will be no plumbing in the Studio. Water will come from snow or from roof rain in Spring/Summer/Fall. The cooking stove: propane gas. Electricity.

The idea is centered on women who need rejuvenating; this will mean creative work or a rest for the psyche. If someone wants to plant a garden and read for four months, so be it. The financial responsibilities are undecided as of now; possibly, if someone sells books or paintings, royalties could help with taxes and upkeep. The "screening" is also up for grabs. Ann Goldsmith mentioned having to have nineteen references, just to see how the person would handle such a request; she and Seashell and I got hysterical one evening talking about nineteen references. Of course, we ended up where we started from: how can you tell what an un-

Lucky and friends on hunt for site, 1977.
Cr: A.G.

known woman is like in the long run? In any case, it's still up for grabs. My own guess is that only one person will be there at a time. It will be interesting to see what actually does happen.

Ann Goldsmith, Pat Hill, Dolores Klaich, and I spoke about women builders. Ann G. is to be the designer and contractor. Ann Wallace knows Doris Hazard — those two will be the major skilled builders. The rest of us will be unskilled labor. Food and lodging are the rewards (my food? eeek!). Ann W. and Doris are $7 per hour.

The four of us, Ann G., Pat, Dolores, and I, walked the land on Easter. When we got too far from the house, Dolores, in desperation, said, "I don't want to carry my groceries this far." Everyone agreed. We ended up at the ledge, about 150 feet from the south boundary, 250 feet from the pole on top of the hill. Moss, big pines, a slope from the ledge downward. It began to feel right.

* * * * *

Ann Goldsmith: An informal Easter weekend discussion among Ann Stokes, Pat Hill, Dolores Klaich, and me regarding the possible construction of a house/studio built by and for women in Stokes's woods.

First step obviously was site location. However, tennis was scheduled. 4:30, chicken feeding. And then, Tour #1 — looking for sites. Lucky Love (cat)

and Wooley Bear (Great Pyrenees) led and followed.
Several possible sites. Future kindling crackled under-
foot. Returned at dusk for a meeting to pull things
together which, by necessity, included a dance record
and drinks.

Long-range plan: a community of women to build
and live. Artists — people planning to live in the community. Immediate: Building #1, a retreat, a haven, a
Studio. Renewing. Not always a "serious" place — fun
and frolic too.

A Studio for a painter, for a writer. To create, to
retreat. Composers. Building for ecological soundness,
i.e., solar heating, et cetera. Divine things:

one stone wall

window seats

open space

a sauna

a soapstone sink

And then there was dinner. As always, a fine repast.

~ ~ ~ ~ ~

One month later . . .

Wow! A chance to put some of the Shelter Institute* knowledge to use, an opportunity to build a real
house. What a terrific way to spend a summer away

*Shelter Institute is a building school in Bath, Maine, which
emphasizes ecologically sound construction.

from Blueberry Cove.* I was so excited about the
prospect, I was afraid to count on it really happening.
It was all in a dream stage when I called Stokie from
the pay phone outside the grocery store in Searsport,
Maine, to find out how she had fared incarcerated in a
New Hampshire National Guard Armory for her partici-
pation in the anti-nuke Seabrook demonstration. She
was fine and very full of the experience, but had
presence to say (toward the end of the conversation):
  "Oh, I have good news."
  "Yes?"
  "George has moved out of the Guest House."
  "Oh? Why is that good news?"
  "Well . . . now there is room for all the women
builders."
  And that is the first time I take the whole idea
seriously. I panic a little, but mostly I am very excited.
The idea of building with an all-women crew does
feel very good, but I begin to be a little worried that I
don't know quite enough or am not quite secure enough
to direct the operation. That feeling is tucked into the
recesses of my mind. I proceed with confidence and
look forward to a glorious summer.
  The idea of what the building ultimately is to be
and who is going to occupy it is so amorphous that I
can't spend too much time on that; I concentrate on

---

*Ann Goldsmith was director of this Maine children's camp
for twelve summers. The camp now offers adult programs, in-
cluding a Women's Building School which grew out of the experiences of working on the Studio on Welcome Hill.

more immediate problems. The design becomes quite simple, universal. Most anyone would like open space and lofts. The shape is pleasing and the structure is such that interior design can be invented later. The drawing board comes from Maine. I retrieve my loaned copy of *From the Ground Up.** I bring my stereo, some work clothes, my toothbrush, and I move into the Guest House.

* * * * *

Ann Stokes: Ann G. decides that running Blueberry Cove for twelve summers needs breathing space. It happens so naturally; her visiting here becomes a summer stay, our first real time together since we were students at Goddard in 1954. We grow into a friendship of warmth and ease; our roots have been nurtured by sky, sun, earth, camping out. She has the dimension of Maine, rocks, sailing. Because she is the only one of us who has studied at the Shelter Institute, the responsibility of designing the Studio falls altogether on her. She lives in the Guest House and designs.

We have begun clearing the site. It took as long to haul the cuttings off into the woods and out of sight as it did to cut them. A few days later, Ann G. crawled from the pole through the woods and underbrush, with

From the Ground Up, by John N. Cole and Charles Wing, Little Brown & Co., Boston, 1976.

Goldsmith clearing Matterbreast Boulevard.

Cr: Seashell

a string in hand, to make a path for the future "road."
It won't be a R-O-A-D, but rather a swath in the woods
for lumber trucks, backhoes,* and other large things
we may need. But its name is grand: The Matterbreast
Boulevard.

[When Dolores first visited Ann one early Spring
and found snow on her steep, curving driveway which
leads to her mountaintop home, she likened the experience (in a moment of lax imagination) to climbing
the Matterhorn, to which Ann replied, "The Matterhorn? This is the Matterbreast!" Like many silly inti-
macies between friends, the name stuck.]

* * * * *

Ann Goldsmith: As May slips into June, before the
crew for the Studio has gathered here, I work with Ann
W. on the chicken house. We work well together, and
I look forward to her return to begin the real house.
Trouble is, I did myself in. In my zeal to be a hard,
good, energetic worker, I knocked my back badly out
of kilter. Days of lying on the floor, doing very little.
A lesson to me. Take it easy!

* * * * *

*See the Glossary for words having to do with the construc-
tion of the Studio.

Ann Stokes: Near the end of June there is a Women's Dance, music by Liberty Standing, scheduled for the Castle, an old ruin in the woods nearby, always referred to by that name. Ann G. and Maggie build a handsome bridge across the pond-stream, and the grounds are tendered to fit a Queen. It pours on the 25th, but the dance goes on at the West Village Meeting House. Wonderful!

The warmth of June rises into the heat of July.

* * * * *

Ann Goldsmith: June sure did slip away hardly noticed, except for the dance—that was very noticeable. I met Jo-Ann Golden there; she is becoming an important person of the summer.

The bridge building and the wonderful dance reruined my barely recovered back and again I was crippled. This time it took less time to recover. When I begin doing heavy work again, later in the summer, I feel I will have developed enough strength and smarts to do it right.

June was a month of clearing land and of making decisions about the Studio's location. I loved going out there day after day, improving the path from the Guest House. I groomed a special pine that was located halfway between the site and the Guest House. That pine was an important tree to me. Early on in June, when I had just begun clearing and looking for the final site,

and I couldn't see how far I was from anything because
of the thickness of the woods, I climbed that pine as
high as I could to see what I would be able to see from
the top of a house that might get built near there.
When that tree got its final pruning, the path took on
a magnificence of its own. I loved that path, always,
remembering how it had once been in that woods and
how it had so slowly materialized into such a fine walkway.

In July, I opened the month with a sudden and
short trip to Wisconsin to visit my family. My brother
Fred was wonderfully supportive of the building project
and listened carefully to the plans. He had helpful suggestions, too, and was glad to let me take some tools
from the basement at Mother's house. But returning
to Welcome Hill and our ambitious project, I became
increasingly uneasy. I couldn't bring myself to order
the lumber, thereby finally committing us to really
doing a design of which I wasn't completely
certain.

I spent time in Putney at Jo-Ann's, getting to know
her and her housemates. They were in the process of
building a post-and-beam addition to their house and
seemed to be so competent and knowledgeable . . . as
well as nice people. I felt very comfortable there very
quickly, and became impatient for our own building to
begin.

Then the idea to get some milled lumber from
Perkins in Keene to build a woodshed hit me. Within
a week, that project began. What a difference it made
to be constructing, measuring, sawing, hammering, and

working out how to do it. It was so good to work with Ann S. too, and so neat to see her delight in learning; yes, we really *can* build a structure.

Then, on a trip to Maine, more confidence suddenly materialized. A friend said he'd been nervous about starting to build, too, but that one simply had to start; changes could be made as one went along. His house was living proof that, Yes, it can happen.

On my return, I bravely ordered gobs of lumber. The foundation was to be put in during the first weeks of August, so we had to be ready to roll.

* * * * *

Ann Stokes: Ann G. and I build a tool- and wood-shed. It is the first time I have built anything in my life. It's wonderful! We rest it on piles of rocks, using levels constantly. Mistakes are made and fixed, and I learn that it is o.k. to make building mistakes. I die at the first ones, but start to relax after the fourth. Ann G. and I work well together. I intuit things and ask her about them; sometimes she has considered them, sometimes not. I am not able to think six steps ahead, but do o.k. on the second and third. I tend to play more; Ann worries tremendously. We notch the small front roof rafters to add a bit of style. This particular notch has another reason — it is the same as the ones on my home and Guest House decks; a way of combining all three structures in unison. Otherwise, the woodshed is a straightforward 8 X 12 structure.

~ ~ ~ ~ ~

"It will take three weeks to deliver the lumber," and we groan. The summer is half finished; Ann G. is getting anxious; the house takes full priority, after a trip to Blueberry Cove. We visit friends in Westmoreland and learn a new way of building footings of stone. They have access to tin for a roof, so we ask them to save us some. The backhoe arrives and hits the ledge very early on. We talk about building footings ourselves, and decide it will take too much time. I call Russell Starkey, and he and his two sons lay footings in one morning! And the foundation in one day!! Gads! "Just put that old cement on the ends of the cinderblocks, like butter, and push 'em next to the block nearest."

With the help of friends we have cut out a path from the top of the hill to the site. I chainsawed the big limbs. They sawed by hand and with the pole saw. Only two trees had to be cut down. Paul Hubner's backhoe just couldn't make it around the very first one, so he pushed it over (HELP) as he pushed over another huge one outside of the "living room window." Paul has greyed also; he looks good.

"What ya got to eat tonight, Stokes?"

"Nothing, Goldenrod."

The woodshed, before and after.   *Cr: A.R.S.*

"Well, I'll see what I have . . ."

"Me, too."

. . . . . "Mmmmm, what a feast!" A summer of corn almost every night; big fat juicy tomatoes. I have eaten well for a change, thanks to Ann G.

* * * * *

Ann Goldsmith: The day the lumber truck came was rainy and dreary. Ann S. was away. Luckily, a friend was visiting and together we unloaded every slab of plywood (60 some in all, I think), and 2 × 10s plus 2 × 6s, and 2 × 8s. Then scads of 6 × 6s were rolled off the truck, landing like pick-up-sticks. Panic, total panic set in. I almost packed up my possessions and disappeared into the sunset. It was very scary. My fear gripped at places I hadn't felt before. I was terrified.

Then, the foundation was completed, on a Friday I think, and Saturday a.m. there was nothing to do but put on the sills. I don't know what it was exactly, but with the first sill in place I began to cheer up. Pretty soon most of the sills were completed and I was figuring out how to put a double 2 × 10 sill down the center; the next thing I knew I was feeling terrific. I had a hammer holster and my work boots — I felt like a pro. I was a carpenter! I was doing it! There was wood in proper places and I could envision the next step — joists! I was strong (I could carry a green

Leveling and then dancing on the first floor joist.
Cr: A.R.S.

12-foot 2 × 10, heavy as hell, by myself); I was competent. I was able to direct people and we, together, were getting it done.

In the middle of it all, I turn forty-four years old. The actual day isn't so significant, but I suspect this summer marks an important crossroad. It has been full of almost every emotion, each strongly felt — the ups and downs severe. When I feel good, it is absolutely terrific; I can do anything, and if it doesn't happen to come out right, tough. When I'm discouraged, nothing can cheer me up. Each of these extremes can happen right on top of the other.

* * * * *

Ann Stokes: The sills went on, with Ann G. and I and others putting on the perfecting touches with the chisel, to make the washers fit tight, the nuts secure. The day had Fall in it, all cool with the sun hot. It clouded in the afternoon, but when the large center piece holding the floor joists went in, the sun shone again.

* * * * *

Ann Goldsmith: A busy day of digging (the dirt inside the foundation needed redistribution), cutting sills, drilling for foundation bolts through the sills, and then getting the center sill supported and notched to fit flush with the sill plates. I demonstrated my dyslexic inability to deal with the visual — what stays and what goes in a notch. I thought it out very carefully and it was exactly opposite. Frustrating. The Studio gets higher and higher, certainly higher than we expected. Now it takes on a realism. It is really there and really happening. Not so scary after today.

* * * * *

Ann Stokes: Seashell arrived at the Perfect Moment; the basement floor had just been hoed and raked into perfection, and it was time to start putting the joists in. There she was, and there she and Ann G. and I worked (I the only one of the crew with shaven pits).

Seashell: The question is: Why does Stokes bother to shave her pits??

* * * * *

Ann Goldsmith: Yesterday, Ann S., Seashell, and I finished the joists, put on the headers, and were ready to start the plywood floor. It must be done by the end of tomorrow. Surely, it will be easy to whap down the eight-penny nails. If you watch a nail carefully as you

Stokes and Goldsmith concentrating.

Cr: Seashell

hit it firmly, you will see it recoil with the impact. It almost looks as if it is going to collapse — not bend, but quakily mush up — but it straightens right up to be smashed again. Nails sure put up with a lot, and then are coffined forevermore in wet, soggy hunks of hemlock. Here's praise to the heroic nail!

* * * * *

Pat Hill: There certainly is a lot of dirt here on the Matterbreast and I seem to have shoveled, hoed, and raked it all from one place to another. We laborers just do what we're told — maybe tomorrow we can saw or nail something (if I can move).

Peanut butter and raspberry jelly sandwiches were served at just the right moment by Ann S. (on an antique tray, of course). She just walked by mumbling to herself, "Nothing's gone up in the air yet." Doris Hazard just walked by saying to herself, "Now I can see it. I couldn't see it last night." Ann G. was just heard from a distance saying, "It's upside down!" (I wonder what was). What an exquisite day this is and what a wonderful spot for a studio and what good feelings surround it.

* * * * *

Ann Stokes: Everything hunky-dory. The rain held off just enough to let the power company give us power.

They were two of the more pleasant men who have come here. Ann G. is happy one day, I am happy the next — one of these days we'll do the jig together, leaping up and down. Doris gives off an air of confidence and competence; she arrived last night into a living room full of ladies. My eyes are blurring with fatigue over All Us Ladies Having Fun.

* * * * *

Ann Goldsmith: Doris and I began the long day today preparing posts. I made some messy notches, but got better by the fourth post and plan to be much more skilled tomorrow. I set up a bedroom on the deck and have spent two glorious nights being the first to sleep in (well, on) the new Studio, guarded by valiant Phoebe (fuzzy, grey cat). We both like it very much, checking out from time to time the position of the moon, the trees in their different night patterns, and early-morning sun catching the tops of the highest pines.

Ann S. and I did an impressive job closing in the toolshed and organizing proper places for all the tools. We sawed and hammered and nailed and measured and figured and said things like, "I am going to buy me my own square," after the nineteenth trip to use the communal one.

* * * * *

Seashell: Raw, golden wood, and very tired faces. Lots of muttering. Mysterious angles and yet more mysterious fractions of an inch that appear on (or vanish from) the ends of heavy beams which one would just as soon not have to re-cut. Everybody's so tired they're shuffling their feet.

* * * * *

Ann Stokes: No Quaker Meeting 'cause them posts and plates was goin' up. But the knee braces! Oh dear, too much air between them and the posts. A good, hot crew of women heaved and put up two plates in weather that made us all droopy. Noises on the site are these: Nanette's panting, hammers on chisels, power saw and power drill, wind in the needles, and conversation here and there. At this very moment, 3 p.m., August 28, 1977, all ten peripheral posts are up and six plates, some knee braces. They are so damn handsome.

Pasta comes for a couple of hours a day, and Pat re-arrived in her new work boots. I am going to mow the lawn.

The first floor of the Studio is much higher than I expected. We need thirty-five yards of fill to improve the sight of the cinderblock. The whole first floor is plumb and secure; Ann G. and Doris finished that yesterday. Ann G. made 16-foot posts which will go up to the roof — they are absolutely stunning. Woweeeee. She is quite a worker.

Chiseling notches, hammering braces.

Cr: Seashell

Doris arrived Wednesday night. Thursday morning Pat, Ann G., and Doris chiseled notches and thought a lot. Seashell and I continued to make the toolshed into a toolshed, with a table and all. The last fittings into the triangular window seemed endless; Seashell really missed in the measuring, and I missed less, but still missed. It took us two days to do it, and within minutes the place was filled with tools.

Cr: A.R.S.

Cr: P.H.

By Saturday, all of us were chiseling and notching, the lumpy earth having been dug and smoothed on the west and north sides. Ann W. arrived Sunday. She and Doris did lots of talking on the site and decided we needed to strengthen certain floor joists for weight distribution. Pasta worked for a couple of hours a couple of days. Pat left on Sunday. On Monday, Ann G., Seashell, Doris, Ann W., and I heaved plates, and by

Cr: P.H.

Tuesday the whole thing was ready for the second story.

Now it is not just the length of Ann G.'s arms which make me pause in amazement; I notice a new tone, a firming of fiber, subtle ripples of muscles being strengthened. A woman's body changing, using what had not been asked of it before. Seashell, an intellectual whose body had been mainly used to carry its head around in the city, has changed quite noticeably — her pale skin has color, she smiles more as the country air hits her grey matter. Not since she was a child has her coordination mattered so. When she uses the circular saw, six weeks into the job, there is assurance in her body. As for me I think my hands have become stronger.

How fascinating it all is, this woman-plus-woman project. *Stretch* is a word that fits. *Bold* is another. Negative competition is visible at times, certainly in me. There are days when I am slower than others, dense in the head, and that bothers me. Some days I am pushed forward by it, on others I accept my slowness. But there are times I am depressed and made insecure by it, when I feel some nasty competitive comparison with others.

Because we dig each other, the bother doesn't fester. And there is the crux of the difference. As diversified a collection as we are, the motive for building the Studio has been felt by each of us in her own way. It is the depth of that cognizance and the individualization of it which is at the core of our wanting to work together. Pat partakes least in the actual building, but her spirit and her suggestions are of the utmost. Her giggles at dinner bring us closer together, without our even knowing why. Her vision of what she wants the Studio to be is keen, presented with gentleness.

Her chiseling for the fittings fits into her personality; she is patient by nature and a perfectionist too, which makes us other lezzies have to care about those 1/16ths of an inch. 1/16th of an inch. For God's sake, it's barely visible! Yet if we didn't take every

damn one into account, the Studio would be out of
kilter. Windows wouldn't fit, skylights would leak,
the whole place wouldn't feel right when you walked
in. All because of not paying excruciating attention to
some barely visible mark on the measuring tape.

Doris's competence is quiet. She is the only builder
by trade on the core crew (she has made her living
this way for eight years; she knows the building would
not only be out of kilter, it would collapse). She is the
opposite of a know-it-all. She answers questions without
a hint of boredom. To watch her work, you think
nothing's being done. Ah, not so! She has her own
grace; it is sprinkled with the toughness of knowing
what must be done.

~ ~ ~ ~ ~

Tail end of August . . . Everyone has left, temporarily. This place, the Matterbreast, is silent. No one
in the Guest House, only the cats Nouschka and Phoebe.
Nouschka seems glad to have some peace again. She is
there, today, whenever I appear, sweetness itself on
four large paws. She is a love and a princess. Hermes
(pussum) has damaged one eye badly. Today is the
first time in five that he has opened it.

I swept the plywood subfloor and dug some earth
into the sanitary land fill. Nanette and Nouschka
stretched out and played on Matterbreast Boulevard.
The day was hot and heavy. It hasn't rained for so

Nanette, 3 months.   *Cr. A.R.A.*

long that the dust puffs over my boottops and into my
socks. The crickets are steady in the evening.

The last dinner with everyone still here was
Scotch, Wild Turkey, and hamburgers with trimmings,
in the lean-to. Doris was laughing a lot and was funny;
we all got silly and tired-giggly. The full moon came
up red over Chesterfield, not a clear knock-out red,
but a slow, heat-hazy red. It seemed to rise quickly.
Time has flown by with all the work and all the ladies.

Ann G. was upset about leaving in general, and
leaving the building in particular. Lots ended so fast.

It is appropriate that everyone has left for a while, giving the house posts and plates a quiet settling in. I, too, need to think other thoughts and do other things. I mowed lawns and paths, cleared under the big pine west of the Guest House, weeded the plants under the sundeck, and freed my old square of its rust. The square is beautiful, the numbers barely visible; I will try my hand at delicately painting some on.

September Uno . . . Another hot one; looked like rain (we need it) in the a.m., but cleared into sun after lunch. My Jeep needed its 92,000-mile checkup, so I

Nouschka.   Cr: A.R.S.

took it in and hitch-hiked home. It was the women who passed me by who made me angry. Finally, a strange, quiet man (tension of *some* sort) took me to Welcome Hill and I walked home from there. The road up the hill seemed shorter than I remembered, but I hadn't done it in a couple of years, and then there had been snow. I picked up a heavy stick to make the drains deeper; it poured one inch in eight minutes in Philadelphia last night; I have grave doubts what my driveway would have done with that kind of onslaught. I was glad I had hitched — a bit of bravery for me.

Waterproofed the sills of the Studio and tool-wood-shed. My guess is they could soak up another application later in the Fall. Daddy-longlegs scooted about everywhere — I dropped many on the ground so their "feet" wouldn't get sticky. Ate a peanut butter and jelly sandwich, drank a root beer, and just gazed at the trees, the Matterbreast Blvd., the Studio.

This is the first quiet time since the beginning. Nouschka, too, has been enjoying the quiet of the site. She and Phoebe tiptoe about each other, N. feeling infinitely better if she is there first. Sitting here today brings nothing specific — I sort of meander in a vague pleasantness until, whammo, the posts and plates become stunning, and I wonder who will work in the Studio, and what she will be like.

In the Adirondacks, my eighty-one-year-old mother became interested in the women's project here. She livened up as if she were fifty again. She paused briefly while she thought of a name we could give ourselves.

Cr: A.R.S.

I.W.W., she said, Independent Wonderful Women.
I love it! She has always risen to the occasion.

~ ~ ~ ~ ~

September 10, 11 . . . Ann G., Seashell, and I dug
two holes under the floor joists for footings which go
under those two beautiful 14-footers in the middle of
the house. Holes had been cut in the plywood subflooring — just letting in enough light for us to see
what we were doing. Digging was less difficult than
we expected. We mixed cement and plopped it into
the holes. Etchings were added for the finishing touch —
one nude lady and the double woman's symbol. Left-
over cement in the bag fired our imaginations. We built
a doorstep in front of the toolshed. At first, the letter-
ing was going to be scratched in, then Seashell thought
of pea-stones, and that's what's there now:
                    BUILT BY
                    I.W.W.
When Seashell looks up at the rising beams, I do
not know what she sees; her gaze takes in much more
than what is before her. There is astonishment, as in
the distant pause of a child taking into itself some
intangible yet large understanding. An expansion
occurs within her concave lovely body — which had arrived bereft and angry from a badly ended relationship.
I am touched by a desperate sadness that has been
brought to the surface by this break-up, the intensity

Cr: A.R.S.

of which can only speak of previous derailments. I want to place the sadness on a down pillow to let it sleep. I myself have been emerging from my own murky forest and want someone to bask in the sun with. I'm not sure she can. I'm not sure how wonderful my own sun is to someone other than me.

She is a loner, unaccustomed to speaking her feelings. They are recognizable in small gestures, a faint
motion of her lip, the way she tilts her head as she
looks at Piero della Francesca. She struggles through
her own preoccupation, trying to take in what others
are saying, not doing very well.

I know why I am struck by her looking at those
beams — it is the first time I have seen her raise her
eyes above sea level.

~ ~ ~ ~ ~

Ann W. and Doris are working hard Wednesday
through Friday. Floor joists are going in quickly. The
place looks fantastic to me. The 6 × 6 posts were put
on our cement footings, and up went the two 14-
footers. Today, the large second-floor joists are being
put in. The weather has been fantastic. Rain falls now,
for almost the first time since we started.

September 19 . . . Doris and Ann W. left last Friday,
and since then the rains have descended. God knows
we need the rain — wells that have never gone dry are
doing so. How well-timed to have it come down when
no one is scheduled to work. The two of them did a
goodly amount of work; almost all of the rafters are
up, as are the 4 × 6 floor joists for the lofts and the
walkway between the lofts, and two of the four top
roof rafters. You can see the spaces and sizes of the
lofts and the part of the first-floor space that will
carry into the roof. I think it looks excellent and

handsome. I had company for four days and then went
to Boston, so couldn't help with the work. Feel badly
about that — mad at the timing of it, but could do
nothing to change things. I feel as though I haven't
worked on the Studio anywhere near the time I want
to. Even knowing there is tons still to do doesn't allevi-
ate my disappointment in not working NOW.

Phoebe is here and has been all along. Nouschka has
really gone — for eight or ten days now. Ann G. returns
tomorrow for a four-day stint, and Doris will come up
also. I have a Civil Liberties retreat Saturday and Sunday, which once again cancels out my working. The
weather has a bit of chill in it today, along with the
heavy rain.

I like having the Studio worked on in clumps; I
couldn't concentrate my whole life on it, day after
day, so am relieved to contend with my psyche and
other parts of my life while everyone is vamoosed. The
long-term perspective has a chance to come alive — I
get excited with the thought of women working there,
feel as though a lot of good work will happen.

* * * * *

Ann Goldsmith: September 25 . . . A certain sadness descends when I pack up more of my stuff and
prepare to leave. Two grey and rainy days halted building and the roof rafters didn't all get up, much less
the roof decking. I feel I am leaving the project for

Designer balancing.   *Cr: Seashell*

good, even though it's just until Spring. There is too much still to do.

I love the high-wire act of drilling for lag bolts to tighten the 4 × 6 rafters. It is scary and I go through periods of panic and moments of being frozen because my weight distribution is wrong, or my direction has to be changed. It feels as though when something has to be done up high, like moving the timber across the joists, I can pick it up and move with no hesitation. Afterwards, I think, My God, that was a scary thing I just did. As the day progresses I get more agile and comfortable. I do hope I will be in on some of the roof decking before winter sets in.

* * * * *

Ann Stokes: October 25, 26, 27 . . . SUNSHINE, balmy weather. Doris moves in, lock, stock, and barrel, to stay and finish the roof decking and siding, come hell or high water. Doris brings books enough to start a little bookstore. We all cook, read, write, talk, and go to bed at different times of the day and night. It's kind of neat. Doris introduced me to Olga Broumas, who is the best poet I've read since Anne Sexton. Nanette is getting older and all of a sudden doesn't want to walk as much. I had her x-rayed to see if her arthritis is worse of if anything else is wrong. The vet's diagnosis: old age. The hens are laying eggs in their new straw mattresses. Pasta's concert is this weekend;

every lesbian from far and wide is expected. Ann G. will return for the concert and will work on the Studio. There should be a huge working crew here.

Today we took off the building braces, and it had the feeling of a special house cleaning. The beams are truly visible now — they are marvelous. A bit of the siding was started on the North wall as the roof was too damp (from midnight mist). The roof decking is about 2/3 finished, as Doris goes over the peak and onto the short side. I have put more fill in and am restacking the battens so they can air and dry a bit. Doing these things while others are working on the Studio is mucho more fun than doing them with no one around.

I am excited to see the Studio "closed in." One month of looking at rafters, however handsome, is long enough, as is one month of sweeping puddles off the plywood.

* * * * *

Doris Hazard: October 31 . . .
 Creating space for women to create
 Space for women to create space
 Home, now, to create in my own space.

* * * * *

Ann Goldsmith: November 1 . . . Having been away from the Studio for a month, I had naturally drifted

Can you find the one who's paying for all this?

Cr: Seashell

Heave-ho!

Cr: Seashell

away from it. The Summer and early Fall were totally immersing — I had thought of little else. I felt a personal loss when I couldn't be involved with each step during some of the Fall. Back to teaching, with all the kids, enjoying the work, and then getting sick (as all teachers do on first getting back to the classroom) were so pre-occupying, I sort of let the Studio go out of my mind.

But coming back last Friday and putting on my hammer holster brought it all back. It felt so good to be measuring, and hammering, and sawing and, most fun of all, prancing about on the roof. It is amazing how one lets go of the fear; slowly one's body and mind adjust to the height. The task takes precedence, and confidence grows out of necessity.

Putting the Studio to bed for the winter is sad, but to think about finishing it in the Spring brings joy.

Two wonderful things about last night's final tasks:

(1) We didn't finish until dark, and then had to clean up. We hooked up a light from the Guest House. What a special feeling to see the light shadowing the Studio as we walked the path toward it.

(2) After I finished the North wall, I found a lovely little wisp of a white pine tree with two equal shoots. I attached it to a board and nailed it on the West peak of the roof. It is our ROOF TREE. The roof tree will protect the building until it is completed. When we build the first woodstove fire, the roof tree will be part of that fire; its ashes will be strewn on the

land from which it was taken. Until then, it stands
proud on the West peak of the Studio roof, waiting
for Spring.

Ann Stokes: May 1984 . . . The work of measuring, sawing, thinking, lifting, and hammering a dream into reality with old and new friends energized me. The first winter, while the Studio relaxed in its own partial completion, I wrote more poems and pieces than I ever had before . . .

Poem

Her back continues on down
separating into long legs.
Her senses shimmer in a
Body that barely holds them,
Seeking a stepping stone
Back to an island which
Holds her beginnings.

Like an island memory she
Is surrounded by water.
Tentative, with the fear of
Being engulfed, she resists comfort.

Finding it in a photograph
Of her own where the tailbone
Of a cow hits its own field
At an exact spot. Holding
For an instant then
Releasing forever that shudder
Of belief.

Passport Photo

It was lovely to have your face
Fall out on the table.
Your nose still crooked
your eyes so large containing their sadness.
But are you tweaking those luscious
Eyebrows?

A little old-fashioned with a floppy
V-neck blouse, you look younger.
The absence of surroundings cannot
hide your perennial annual you-name-it
Beauty.

Are you going somewhere? To see me?
Ah, but your letter did not fall on
The table; was very stay-at-home,
Responding to the news I mailed

With feet firm, seat ensconced.
You are not going to take a trip.

I enclose myself, via glossy
Snapshot, to you, my long-time
Far-away sweetheart.

March

The grove was handsome today.

Sitting on a pile of logs
My windjacket partly open to Spring
Partly closed to Winter that was
At once staying and leaving.

The light changed quickly
To dark deep grey. Sudden snow
Whirled about in a wind
Rushing from the tops of the trees
Down trunks. Thick swirls
Racing about, the light from
Their whiteness seductive.

Chaotic in its wildness
Caring only for their own joy
The Spring flakes were saying
To hell with cold drab
Winter flakes bake a cake
Dance to the tune of mulberry trees
and Greek frieze.

The heat of power — the fingertips
The lungs. The feet. The brain.

Clearing

I work in my woods as I live my life — I like to come upon things. I am clearing space around one of the pines that meant something to me fifteen years ago: the big one just past the two oaks. I am thinning with most of my outdoor tools — chain saw and clippers. Two afternoons have been spent here. Today, the third, I used the chain saw to fell the thicker young maples and take off the bottom limbs of another few pines nearby.

I sit down. As the sweat cools I look around at what has been finished and what still needs to be done. A large mass of white fur takes the corner of my eye as she dozes on the brown pine needles. There are the little wildflowers I have put stones around. A bramble has found good soil; it is big. A rock of quartz is uncovered. The one massive root (it looks like a partially buried branch) appears again. So many things I have forgotten since the underbrush took over.

A certain trail in the Adirondacks whooshes into my vision. I remember a dream of wild horses galloping. "Grand, muscley names" glow in that part of the brain near my heart. I see the profile of the woman I love as she talks to my mother.

I go back home for lunch.

Returning to work I walk along a path with hemlock, pine, cherry, and weeds on both sides, suddenly breaking out into this new clearing. It is not large. I pause with delight — my own — then wonder if the birds will be glad to have a brief second of flight in which they don't have to worry about limbs and twigs and the vine that sprawled itself upward.

It is fall. The afternoon light hits the trunk of the tree with a wallop. The bark shines. The limbs seem grander. Each needle is defined. The form is full of an energy it did not seem to have in the summer. The whole tree gives forth the effort it took to become that size. It makes itself known.

Ann Stokes: Throughout the Winter I had trundled over just to look at the Studio. It seemed so large. Here's what we had accomplished: the posts and beams were completed; the roof decking was on; the subflooring was in; the North wall was finished. Most dreams involve psychic changes, insights, and resonances. Here, before me, was a physical structure, a different dream outcome. As I stood before it, I thought of how well we women had worked together, how the impetus to build for unknown artists had sparked that special connection to each other. Pettiness was at a minimum throughout those working weeks. Most of us had never thought of ourselves as carpenters. I had known Pat Hill and Ann Goldsmith each for twenty-five years. They, in turn, became friends, giving double depth to the project.

During the Winter, I swept snow off the plywood flooring, and with my pole saw I took off more tree limbs so the eye could travel deeper into the forest. The structure nestled into its surroundings and rested until Spring. Time went by quickly. Soon, I called the crew, those Independent Wonderful Women, to see when we could assemble.

* * * * *

Doris Hazard: April 5, 6 . . . I arrive with a truck-load of insulation, tools, food, clothes, and ladders. I shovel snow off the roof, about a foot in some places. Seashell builds a ladder to the second floor — it is beautiful and it works. Seashell and I build scaffolding on the South side to the roof. The first time back after months of non-carpentry takes some adjusting.

Ann S. and Joan Hamilton put up the siding on the center bay of the South wall; Seashell does the siding on the North end of the East wall (in the kitchen area).

I put in an order to Smead:

> 2 rolls roofing (for woodshed)
> 5 lbs. roofing nails
> 10 sq. white shingles
> 50 lbs. 3-inch roofing nails
> 2 gallons roofing cement
> etc.

Cr: P.H.

My saw breaks; much frustration and a slower pace.
A warm, sunny day — good to be working outdoors.
    April 7 . . . Snow! Oh! Spent most of the day get-
ting parts for my broken saw. To Brattleboro, then to
Keene. Finally, success at 1 p.m. Little work by me.
Cold and damp at 6 p.m. Best thing to do is drink a
cold beer and soak in a hot tub.
    April 8 . . . Ann S., Joan, Seashell, and I continue
to work on siding. The Studio gets closed in more
and more. Time to put in some skylights!

                            * * * * *

    Ann Stokes: Seashell leaves for a short trip to the
big city to catch up on friends, to see about work
projects, to get her cat back to her own home. The cat's
been living here in the bedroom and bathroom, with oc-
casional forays into the living room to face hisses and
some bad noises. She survived the experience, bouncing
through the fluffs of the down comforter to our love
and pats. She ate on the third day, finally! Much worry-
ing went on about her. Sweet puss.
    Seashell worked very hard, doing most of the East
wall, which looks beautiful. Also, a good part of the
walk space upstairs. Joan and I helped put up some
of the South wall; I helped Seashell with the East wall.
Doris put up all the window frames, and some scaffolding, which looks enormously precarious to me, but
it holds her.

The weather has been damp and cool essentially, with two beautiful, sunny days interspersed. Still the need for long underwear, two sweaters, and a vest. One day there was a Spring snow which looked so lovely outside the kitchen "window."

Half of my garage houses the skylights and the roof insulation for the Studio. The West wall is getting plywood under the boards and battens to help against the cold winter winds. Today, Pat and Doris and I cut out an oddly shaped new window in the West wall. It helps make the wall more interesting, from the outside in particular. Doris had almost cut through a smaller space in the plywood when we came and changed the whole thing.

I climbed to the top to hammer, but each time something wouldn't work; I hadn't hammered the nails in the right place; then Pat's smaller ladder was in the way, then I started to feel skittish (speaking of unskilled labor, I couldn't have felt more so!). Finally, Doris climbed up and Did It. I did some work where it wasn't so high.

Wedging is one of the neatest, most satisfying things to do. Pushing the board over to make it fit snugly by simply whacking a wedge between a block of wood and the board, is one of the simplest delights I've ever come across.

The stairs problem was taken on by Seashell, who presented it before the Board of Doris and Pat. The three of them talked a long time until it was figured out. The stairs will be straight up, starting from a rise to the right of the front door. Seashell probably will

Cr: P.H.

make them, as it interests her so. We had traveled from
a spiral stairway, to the walkway, to this. I am tickled
with the solution. Spiral staircases don't interest me at
all, and the simplicity and straightforwardness of this
straight-up decision makes me smack my lips.

I haven't really plunged into the work the way
I want to yet — the Land Trust Annual Meeting* on
Sunday, plus appointments on Monday, excluded me
two whole days. But I have changed from last summer
when my work was mucho sporadic. Now, I really
want to participate and learn.

*The Earth Bridge Community Land Trust, Putney, Ver-
mont, is a co-operative venture formed to use the land wisely;
A.S. is on the Board.

In the week of solid work Seashell did, her body tone changed. Her face got color; by Monday night she really looked wonderful in that way working in the outdoors brings. Pasta was going to help again, until she heard my rate for unskilled labor — she almost fainted on the phone when I told her. This weekend, the roof with the skylights goes up. Ann G. comes to help and stay for a week.

Skylights, insulation, and asbestos shingles. We decided on white shingles, to reflect the sun. Also, the roof is not very visible, so it doesn't matter very much what's there.

Jane Stone suggested as one of the questions for potential artists: "How do you *know* the Hawaiian Islands exist?"

Doris guesses the custom-made window will cost $100; she bases this on the cost of a normal window and adds fifty percent. The velux skylights are Gorgeous, Handsome, and EXPENSIVE.

April 16 ... Yesterday the smaller (South) side of the roof was insulated with 2-inch Styrofoam, tar-papered and asphalt-shingled — all on *one* cold windy *day*. There was a big crew. Doris spent time putting the chimney in, Seashell and Ann G. did the heavy hauling up the BIG LADDER — pounds of shingles and every other needed object that weighed anything. It snowed peculiar Styrofoam snow from time to time; the sun-blessed-sun came out occasionally; in the last two hours of the day the roof just zoomed to its finish. I couldn't believe how conventional it looked and also how professional. Doris started it

Cr: P.H.

all, standing on her scaffolding — she alone (thank
God), hammering in the metal edging and the first
shingles which come 3-in-1. That was news to me. I
thought we would be hammering them in one by one.
The whole Studio shook when Joan walked across
the roof. Mostly it was cold cold cold; there was much
more tension than I had anticipated. After a bath I
just zonked off to sleep for a couple of hours. The
evening was lovely — dinner at the Saxton's River
Inn.

Doris and Ann G. did more window framing in
the morning. The rest of the roof needs two long
days — skylights et al. Seashell and I had a Sunday
Sunday — the *New York Times* after Quaker Meeting.

Then Seashell zonked out as I had yesterday. Later, a feast of roast beef and avocado salad. Reading, writing, and Othello took over what was left after feasting.

* * * * *

Ann Goldsmith: The past two days back on the job have been wonderful. Feels really good to be climbing along the joists, toenailing window framing, edging cautiously toward the edge of the 18-foot drop from the roof, saying FUCK KNOTS when the nails wouldn't go in, and figuring out things. There is an ease on the job. Tension has vanished for me. There is real satisfaction in seeing all that's been done. Yesterday, walking up from the driveway with a load of 2 X 6s, I thought about a year ago when the project was conceived and how much had changed along that boulevard. The piles of cut logs along the road are a monument to the weekend we first cleared the woods. Now a handsome building stands proudly at the end. And next April? It will again be altogether different, with more history and wonderful memories.

* * * * *

Doris Hazard: Rain and more rain. Ann G. and I put in decking on the lofts. She builds stairs — she can't resist. They are fun to build and feel much better than the little aluminum ladder we used to do all the truckin' on. I start work on the framing for the skylights. We both hope for sunny clear skies.

* * * * *

Ann Stokes: Sunshine, sunshine, SUN-with-heat-in-it up there on the roof. Missed Pat a bit on this lovely Spring day. I saw only small patches of snow in the woods when Pooch and I went for our early morning walk. Seashell put in the framing for the second chimney way up there in circus tent space, no net under her, balancing on a sawhorse set on top of planks which were on another temporary cross beam — a wobbly edifice to be on at all, let alone when hammering in nails at a most peculiar, precarious angle. Tension in the legs and the constant frustration of having only "one" hand, the other needed for balancing.

Ann G. and Doris are cutting four large rectangles in the roof for the skylights. We all spent much time deciding where they should go. After the decision was made and the cutting was done it seemed odd that there had been anything to discuss, so right and simple it all seemed. And yet — How much light should be in the upstairs studio? Is one skylight enough? Should there be more light shining into the downstairs? How will they look if they're all in a row, if there is a space between them? And should we keep on ordering more skylights, since they are so neat?

Golden.   *Cr: Nancy Gonchar*

Tuesday Seashell and I came up with a plan for the closet and bathroom. How not to make them look like odd boxes sticking out from the North wall was one large problem. The kitchen remains where it always was planned to be, in the corner. Next to it is the library nook; it will have lush carpeting, books, an old upholstered chair, and one lamp. It's the hermit spot, even though it opens into the living space. The bathroom and a closet, which will have their common wall snug to the staircase, finish out the North wall, leaving room for coats to hang and boots to dry. It

Seashell.   *Cr: Nancy Gonchar*

took a good hour to work that one out. Pat may come along and have other ideas.

Tomorrow I wheelbarrow the rest of the Matter-breast around the foundation. And when Doris returns on Tuesday we make a leetle trip to the dump — the grounds are very messy.

The crew of Ann G., Doris, Seashell, me, eat like horses. Sweets, meats, vegetables, teas, and coffees just travel down the old gullet like rain down a gutter. Many baths, some Scotch; what wonderful workers we are. What lingers in my mind: Ann G.'s imitations of racing cars, hissing cats, loud bumps (sounded on a slightly lesser key by me), Doris's mellow chuckles, Seashell's city muscles stretching in the country air, her tits lilting on the rooftop as the sun hits them for the first time this year. Pat has been absent these past few days, off in Philadelphia again.

* * * * *

Ann Goldsmith: Maggie and I are here for the weekend. After a trip to Putney and Westminster West to look over the building wonders of others we returned to almost finish the South wall siding. I cut boards and Maggie skillfully nailed them in place. The highlight of the short work period was Maggie's putting up of the last board, nailing from the inside. The space to reach around had become narrower and narrower as we got closer to the West wall. Finally only Maggie's arm fitted through. She put the last two nails in by feel, giving birth to a new field we dubbed blind carpentry.

My back has given way. Badness!

* * * * *

Seashell: May 11 . . . Long and lazy lapses. We put in two windows, framed in one. Doris sanded and

primed the bookshelves, trimmed gobs of tarpaper
from the roof, finished a drip edge on the windows.
Ann S. temporarily lost a window handle and tripped
several times on the mysteriously raised floor in the
upstairs bedroom. BLACKFLIES in abundance, hang-
ing in clouds. They like Pat best, lucky for the rest
of us.

* * * * *

Ann Stokes: Doris has left. She's off to England!
To meet her love, do carpentry, see a gay bar or two,
go to the Hebrides. So, a bright and very knowledgeable
light has flown the Studio, leaving the rest of us to
make do. Right now all hands to the studding so the
rough wiring can be put in before the insulation.

Memorial Day weekend finds Pat using the Studio,
incomplete as it is. She is slicing, at a most gorgeous
angle, some green boards for the garden that will feed
us. The past days we have been concentrating on studding. Lesley Straley comes three days a week, Seashell
five.

Seashell and I put the red roof on the woodshed
today. It had been very neglected, with tarpaper flap-
ping in the breeze and plywood taking many raindrops.
The red rolls of asbestos were absolutely handsome.
Doris ordered the correct amount to a T. Simple as
pumpkin pie to put it on.

Summer has come. It is sunny and hot with a big

thundercloud out the West window. Heat has made us tired. Showers and beer help.

I cleared out the henhouse yesterday, putting in fresh wood chips, opening the winter window to allow airing. We are sending photos of huge mansions to Doris in England, pretending they are shots of the Studio. Today the last of the bedroom floorboards took a stubborn kick — the grooves would not fit around the tongues no matter what we did. I stood on them, Seashell hammered, and still they said no. Frustrating. We finally had to chisel off the tongues.

Jacques Jarvis will do the wiring and Mark Firestone the sheetrock. Deviations! Men! Oh dear! But none of us want to do the sheetrock with all the care it entails; we haven't found other women willing to take it on. And the one female electrician we know is busy on another job.

Totaled up the cost so far: $13,000. Largest outpouring for lumber, the next for labor. Not bad, I think.

Now that the weather is summering in we consume huge amounts of liquids. Lesley brings sweet apple cider, Minute Maid brings endless amounts of orange juice. Ice water, V-8, ginger ale, all go down the hatch. The power saw began smoking the day after Seashell dreamt that some pine needles caught fire and were quickly put out. I will get a fire extinguisher next week. So far we laborers are good at figuring out what has to be done without Doris's able help. Seashell has taken on the major responsibility for comprehension. Ann G.'s back has her out flat in Boston. She is

trying to accept that it will be a long haul. It's strange
not to have her popping in.

* * * * *

Seashell: Today was aggravating — boards not fitting — grrrrrr!

* * * * *

Ann Stokes: Seashell has become a full-fledged
carpenter today: she constructed a door from scratch.
It is a very very very fine bathroom door, which now
slides by way of a runner at its top. Lots of thought
went into making it right. The bathroom feels private
now. It's a rather delicate door, really, and ever so
much nicer than the solid plain one in the Guest House.
Lesley and I studded more on the East wall upstairs.
She was in a funny mood; we sang old-time hymns,
stole the level from Seashell as often as we could. Seashell feels very good about her door. As well she might.
    Nanette joined us in the Studio. She is getting older
and is in need of constant companionship. Mark will
do the sheetrock in about three weeks. Possibly we
can have an insulation party with as many ladies as
possible stapling away.

* * * * *

Seashell: Late June. Everybody has been working so very hard, so very diligently, that no one has had enough surplus energy to move a pen across a blank page. However, today was an exception: a wall got done, therefore more adrenalin. It looks good.

A man, despite Ann S.'s adamant injunctions of last Fall, is hammering nails into the sheetrock. He is very nervous about all the ladies. He makes mistakes when the women help. Once he sheetrocked over an outlet. Now he is very tentative and polite about requesting help. There must be a moral to this story. No deck footings yet. Walls are slow and maddening.

* * * * *

Ann Stokes: The long hours which turned into days of studs have paid off: we are now putting up walls. Lesley and Seashell and I spent three days putting up the bedroom wall. It looks absolutely stunning. Lesley has had to leave us to work in a summer music camp. I miss her.

Mark has finished putting up the sheetrock and has been taping the seams and nails. Jacques has finished the wiring. Mark is really having a reaction to us ladies: whenever we get near him he measures very badly or forgets to put in holes for the electric outlets. Seashell and I happened to be insulating in the bedroom where he was to put up the last piece and he said,

"I've got to run now." I don't know if it's women in general or us lezzies, but he gets totally discombobulated. Strange! Today I was in Boston and he had the space to himself. Lots got done.

* * * * *

Headline from the *New York Times*, June 26:

20,000 GATHER AT SITE
OF SEABROOK NUCLEAR PROTEST

Ann Stokes: The whole crew decided that on June 25 we would shift from measuring to demonstrating. We took off for Seabrook, New Hampshire, to join in protesting the nuclear power plant there. The year previous, I had been arrested with 1,413 others in a non-violent civil disobedience action against the plant based on ecological, military, and every other grounds you can think of. This day was to be one of demonstration only.

Twenty thousand of us gathered under a permeating sun. In the midst of Arlo Guthrie's singing I saw my older sister in a safari-like outfit administering water, juices, and salt tablets. A nurse by profession, she was in her element here. I watched her move with grace and sureness — from one to another — a bit of Carole Lombard there. Never had I seen her so beautiful . . . and I suddenly remembered how attracted I had been when I was eleven, she seventeen, how intense and brief that moment had been, how it had resulted in a fear that had knocked the beauty from my beholder's eye until now, thirty-six years later. Two sisters, once together, now apart in our lives, had chosen to stand against the devastating risk of nuclear power. She tall and blonde, I shorter and brown — no one would guess we were mothered and fathered by the same two. A younger sister's eyes still in awe, in such an unexpected place! The family portrait had lost its luster over the years, but the tie that day was rejuvenated. No matter what we can't say to each other grown-up, the link once there has not been broken.

There was someone else on the podium when I returned from my reverie and found myself part of the crowd again. I said to Pat: The anti-nuclear protesters are no longer few — we have become a movement.

Headline from the *New York Times*, July 1:

U.S. ORDERS A HALT
TO WORK AT SEABROOK

* * * * *

Ann Stokes: July 20 ... A hot, sultry non-Studio day. They found the septic tank for my house today. For anyone building a house: do record where the tank is; stupid kinds of energy will be spent looking for it.

Our major semi-skilled carpenter, Seashell, will soon be leaving. It is wonderful to see what can happen

to a person who hammered in nails crookedly in May
and is now doing finishing work like rounding the edge
of the last board on a wall and flushing it with a beam.
Cozy and rather handsome, I must say.

We are both eager to be outside; yesterday we
dug the last four holes for the deck footings; tomorrow
we'll pour the cement and then put up the biggies.
Seashell has begun the large wall downstairs which
has spilled up to the working studio, surrounding the
bookcase on the South wall and the South small
window. The finishing makes the windows suddenly
look like something — cared for, mainly. Lots of things
are pulling together. Mark has finished the sheetrock.
We will prime and paint. But it's the walls that are
so wonderful — the ship-lap walls.

The closet is finished, ready for a light. Jacques
is waiting for us to get all the fixtures so he can hook
them up.

Work on the Studio is totally up to Seashell and
me now — whenever a gap needs closing, a room asks
to be finished, a decision for rough or smooth ship-
lap needs to be made, horizontal or vertical, inside
or outside . . . I'm TIRED OF looking at INSULATION.
The whole place is now insulated; all that remains to
be done is the crawl space under-flooring, our great
avoidance. There is so much yet to be done that we
vary from day to day, week to week. For weeks I
was buggy about the horizontals on the back of Doris's
upstairs bookcase. Finally, Seashell was getting buggy
about them too so last week they went up. We wonder
about Doris's reaction from time to time. I can't wait

for her to return and look things over. Still no 3½-inch roofing nails.

* * * * *

Seashell: MUCH TOO SWELTERING HOT to lift a finger . . . but corn and tomatoes and basil are here.

Looking out dining room window.   *Cr: P.H.*

FALL / WINTER
1978

Ann Stokes: September 13 ... The end of the process is now in sight. We primed all the downstairs sheetrock yesterday and today. The place looks suddenly finished. I ordered a composting toilet, scheduled to arrive next week. Will it fit through the bathroom door? Almost all the lighting fixtures are in place — and I am broke. Just took out a loan for $5,000 ... Squeezin' by.

It seemed funny working all summer without Doris. She is such an energy. Seashell was the most constant worker, with Lesley and myself joining in. Jo-Ann came for an important two weeks in August. She and Seashell did the circular back deck, not an easy undertaking. They and Lesley took half a day figuring out how to find the center of the circle. The

73

The deck.   *Cr: Nancy Gonchar*

deck makes that corner of the Studio into an absolute
joy. I don't think it needs a railing. Let it remain free
floating. Yummers.

The flooring arrived the other day. It is absolutely
gorgeous maple. Lesley and I stacked what looks to be
enough for two studios. She covered it with obsessive
care. I liked that.

October 9 . . . Doris is back! She and I started
making holes in the ceiling and roof for the exhaust
of the Mullbank, which is certainly one of the better
looking composting toilets. It even came with a bag
of peat moss from Sweden. I like it! You step up
to it. I used the saber saw for the ceiling and roof
cutting. Broke two blades in the process. Also touched

the blade after I had been using it, burning my soft fat fingertips. Maybe my second saber outing will be better.

Lesley continues with her persistent perfectionism. It makes the walls *superb*. But when a crack doesn't get less cracky she does tend to go on a bit into the forever. Doris works deceptively quickly and onwardly all day long; she is wonderful. Jo-Ann came back on the scene today, possibly to take Doris's place. Doris has been pushing herself to come here between the beginnings of her own house, and she would like to get back there. So she and Jo-Ann will come to a decision tomorrow. I will miss her, but Jo-Ann is good to work with and very competent (just have to turn down that radio volume from time to time).

Maple is hard; laying a floor is hard. It moves slowly. Hammering in the wedges, asking for some added weight (me, to be specific) when needed, getting the 3″, 4″, 5″ boards in the right row and the right length, covering where the joists lie hidden. Just finding the joists to begin with!

Ann G. arrives this weekend with a friend. If all goes well, the floor will be finished by the time she arrives. God, how exciting! I do hope she loves the place with which she once was so involved — that her sadness about her bad back doesn't dampen her excitement.

Tale of the water storage tank . . . I siphoned out (after learning how to suck hard enough) the water storage tank, which is in the upstairs studio. It needs to have an overflow hole and pipe made. Last weekend

it rained. It rained hard Friday afternoon and water
from the roof gutter poured into the tank, filling it
1/3 full. Then it rained hard Monday night. At 4:30
a.m. Doris decided she just better go see what was
going on. She got there, peered in, and found the
water 3 inches from the top. She removed the roof
gutter, but Lordy that was close. And we were worried
about water supply!

October 15 . . . A landmark day, yesterday. The
Studio was moved into by its first occupant, Lesley
Straley by name, a violinist by profession, a carpenter
when need be. She brought her plants, pots, pans,
bedding, et cetera, and just lay down to sleep.

The work continues. The West wall battens were
finished last week after Lesley and Jo-Ann framed
the big door and window. It was fun working with
Jo-Ann and doing battens again. Jo-Ann took the
kitchen sink to her workshop in Putney, and will
build the kitchen counters that flank it. Lesley got
the Mullbank "on its feet" — so far, it is just fine.
It takes leaves, cut grass, and sawdust for its composting needs. The firewood lies waiting for a stack-
ing party.

It is wonderful to look down the Matterbreast
Boulevard from the trapezoid window inside the Studio,
especially when Nanette is lying by the big tree. That
was my first look, with her there.

Today is Patricia Prudence Hill's forty-third birthday. She is in New York City at Janet Flanner's
memorial service. Flanner died at eighty-six of a heart

Nanette, 9 months.

attack; the *Times* had a wonderful photo of her, taken very recently. Such a lady!

Lesley is a bit aggravated by flying sawdust as Jo-Ann continues with the finishing work. But she will have quiet during the Winter months until Spring when we start the last of the projects: the permanent staircase, bookshelves for the nook, window seats under the corner windows, a gutter on the South roof, stairs to the back deck, and benches for it.

In the meantime, the Studio has its first stayer, an artist who is also a builder. Fitting.

PART II
THE ARTISTS
OF THE STUDIO

Pat Hill
Pat Staten
Judy Stein
Dohrn Zachai

Cr: P.H.

Judy Stein: September, 1980 . . .

From the very beginning I loved this space. Coming
into it that first day, warm patches of sunlight greeted
me; I saw a variety of places to please my different
moods. The first working day I cuddled up in the reading alcove. The second day, feeling more secure, I spread
out into the larger, more open work area upstairs. Everywhere there is evidence of caring; most details have
been attended to with a loving, zany spirit — the large,
ornate iron handle to the back door, for example.

Tonight I took the logbook to bed and spent an
hour reading the entries and scrutinizing the photos
showing the early stages of construction. It was like
looking at a friend's family album — knowing her
now as an adult, I take special pleasure in seeing old
photos which record her babyhood, and enjoy searching her young features for resemblances to the present.

I feel cradled in the dreams and love that went
into the building of this Studio, nurtured by the

Cr: P.H.

commitment of its *construction*. Sappho would be very pleased to learn that in *this* space I am charting the fluctuations of her reputation in *posterity*.

October, 1980 . . .

I have been so consistently happy up here in my little house in the woods, so delighted with my solitary (mostly) existence. Oh, I know the novelty has yet to wear off, but I'm not so blindly romantic as to have idealized this way of being. It suits me so — the quiet, the proximity to an unspoiled forest, the pacing out of my work and my day without the world intervening.

The only enemy is me, and I'm getting to know myself better. In fact, the only analogy (or description) I have for the way I feel is to say that I'm in love (high) on/with myself. I remember feeling this way before only in response to another's love — their interest made me feel better and be more appreciative of myself. Here, there is just me, and although I went through a few days of intense erotic fantasies (well, I *am* writing the "sexiest" chapter of my thesis) I really am not up for the intensity of sexual contact with another person.

I'm already fearing my re-entry trauma which, of course, must happen to some extent when I return to being a wife, mother, friend, radio reviewer, opening-goer, feminist community busybody, etc. My wall, which exists by the very isolation of this place, will no longer exist. In Philadelphia I will (must) build my own artificial wall to keep the world out until I am awarded that wonderfully horribly grand Ph.D. in December DO IT!

* * * * *

Dohrn Zachai: I was at Welcome Hill twice for stays of about three weeks, and about four years apart. Each stay was a digestion time for profound changes in my life and art, rather than primarily a time of work.

The few years in advance of my fiftieth year I had elaborate goals based on twenty-five years committed to fiber sculpture. For one thing, I was going to make the BIG AMERICAN TAPESTRY! That ambition and the body-mind-artist began to pull apart.

At the beginning of this crucial transition and again toward the end — like parentheses around a wordless sentence — I was protected by the virgin walls of the Studio, virgin to me because no vestige of my past art or life was visible. I thought of my time there in terms of the vision quest of the Native American. On a less spiritual level, it felt like a mental haven especially created for my particular brand of crazy: A Woman and an Artist in the (to me) unsupporting culture of USA–NOW.

This mid-life turnabout was solidified by my un-challenged acceptance at the Studio, a transitional refuge which appeared to be an unplanned answer to an unvoiced need. I say this because I cannot re-call how it all came about. It was an extraordinary gift to a person always perplexed by the present (tense, that is; pun unintended). The wonder of Ann Stokes's handling of the Studio is most apparent when I think of the complicated, over-intellectualized proposals and proofs of validity encountered in applications for other grants and residencies.

Dhorn Zachai in the Studio.

Welcome Hill is the only place I have inhabited (outside of museum visits) where the importance/ acceptance and the making of art is not an aberration, but a necessity requiring a special quality of shared privacy and solitude. The power of a "place" on my development, and knowing it is servicing others, quadruples my power as artist and woman. The place, the fact of a mountain given over to women creating, is an affirmation to me as large as the National Gallery of Art.

As my fiftieth birthday rolled over almost unnoticed, work/life/priorities had shifted from the ambitious, goal-oriented artist working in an experimental medium, to an artist working from a commitment derived from love, with the process/challenge researched/enlarged/experimented with more directly from our Western painting heritage. With minimum fuss and materials, out under the sky as much as possible, working with and from the earth and sky.

A conversation with Ann comes to mind. I was questioning the relevance of making pastels (making my own colors from dry pigment and drying the sticks in the sun), at a time when I felt the earth on the edge of catastrophe. Ann said with perfect clarity, "Making pastels is an ACT of peace." The complex simplicity of that remark remains with me a year and 1500 miles distant.

* * * * *

Pat Staten: I thought, "This is a shed. It has to be some kind of shed or something." The rent was $100 a month. With a figure like that, I was convinced I was going to see someone's converted chicken coop. But I was desperate for a place to work outside of New York City. I had just finished four months at Yaddo and the MacDowell Colony.

A year before, a friend who was at MacDowell told me about a notice on the bulletin board for a studio, rent $100, with an unbelievable description. I called Ann Stokes, but the Studio was taken. I didn't believe her description. I kept seeing rags stuffed between rotting boards, torn screens and cracked

Looking down the stovepipe.   *Cr: P.H.*

windows. A year later, at MacDowell, I realized my
playwriting project wouldn't be completed and I
couldn't yet face New York, so I called Ann again

and she said the Studio was available. I drove over to
see it.

Ann walked with me to the site, with an escort
of two dogs and one cat who, I was sure, understood
my desperation and willingness to take anything that
kept the rain out. When I first saw the Studio and Ann
indicated that that was it, I thought she really meant
the woodshed beside it.

We went in and I was knocked out. The skylights,
the wood floors, the space, the open, fresh feeling
and finally — what this writer's dreams are made of —
a large desk by a window. I kept searching the place
for a hitch. Did the stove really give off enough heat?
Would I spend the winter huddled in front of it? Did
the compost toilet really work? (This gave me strange
visions.) Were the logs piled up outside genuine or a
prop? Were the dogs real? Was the cat bugged?

I couldn't find the catch. I decided to take it.
Otherwise, I might have to go back into therapy again.

I was in the Studio nine months. I had good periods
and bad periods with the writing. During the good
periods, it was a dream come true. The quiet and no
distractions. I grew up in Kansas, and since then nature
and I have not been on the best terms. However, there
were times some of my old awe of nature returned —
watching a snow storm, trees encased in ice glittering
in morning light, birds, stars, the northern lights which
I saw for the first time. It was reassuring to know
it was all still there, going on as it should. One has
doubts living in the city.

I brought my cat up from New York. She'd never

seen anything green. She attacked the grass when she
first saw it. After that victory, she retreated inside
again. It took her six months to realize she was in
the country. When she did venture outside, she was
happy to crush one flower by the door and stalk the
car. In the city she threw up every time the telephone
rang. The vet said she was high strung. She didn't throw
up when the telephone rang in the Studio. I never
figured that one out. She only threw up when I opened
the back door or slept past ten in the morning.

In the summer, I left the front door open slightly
so the cat might get the idea there was something out
there besides muggers and garbage. One night I was
in bed, in the "nest" (second floor bedroom), reading
Nightwood for the first time. It was about two in the
morning and I only had one light on over the bed.
As I was reading, I thought I saw something fly by.
I decided I had to be more objective about this book.
About ten minutes later something whizzed by again
pursued by my cat. The cat gave it reality. I wasn't
hallucinating. It was a bat. It had probably come in by
way of the door I had left open for the cat.

When I realized it was a bat, I freaked. Visions
of rabies and Dracula. Five hours of *Nightwood*. I
called Jane in the Guest House. Jane said she'd be
right over. She appeared wearing a large orange hat.
We spent several hours chasing the bat around with a
broom, drinking, and telling of previous bat or bat-like
encounters and praying to the Hopi Indians for spiritual
guidance. I called a friend in New York City for help.
She suggested we shoot the bat. That didn't seem

Artist Angela Muriel and her workspace.

Cr: P.H.

possible. We opened the skylight and finally the bat got the idea and flew out. The cat threw up.

Aside from this, I had no dramatic adventures at the Studio, and that was the beauty of it. No drama. No distractions. I enjoyed the uneventful days of quiet and isolation and watching the change of seasons which I had not seen in fifteen years. In New York, I know spring has arrived when the population of muggers increases. I continue in my love/hate relationship with the city.

I don't think there's anything more important for any artist than to have a place to work, to simply have the peace and time to work. It is, by far, the most

Cr: P.H.

difficult problem for every artist I know. Just to be left alone to work in a good environment. It is a blessing to have a place like the Studio.

* * * * *

Pat Hill: Painting, working at it consistently, has never been easy for me. The juggling of time spent making money to keep body and cat together, with

Lucky.
Cr: P.H.

actual woman-hours spent putting something on canvas, has always left me feeling rather like Alice in Wonderland, running and running and never catching up. And as if that weren't enough reason to paint rarely, I've had my own demons to wrestle — laziness, fun always waiting to be had, and that oldie-but-goodie, fear of success.

Artist and visitors: Pat Hill, Simone and ChoCho
Cr: Joan Meyers

And so it was, replete with all these bad habits, but bent on restoring faith in myself as a painter, that I left Philadelphia and went to stay with my oldest and dearest friend, Ann Stokes, in the winter (and I do mean WINTER) of 1978. And I might add, like all good lesbians of the '70s, I went with a severely broken heart and burn-out from throwing myself against the bastions of homophobia once too often.

Ann had always been able to fix anything before,

in the twenty years I'd known her, but psychically, I was a "necessitous case," as they say in Quaker circles, and it seemed a lot to ask of her. There really wasn't much left of me at all when I arrived that February, in a blizzard, with my three cats and all my belongings. Like the Woman Who Came To Dinner, I came for three months, and stayed three years on that exquisite, seductive mountain in New Hampshire, working for six months in the Studio. In that time I not only repaired but had one of the richest experiences of my life.

Epilogue

Ann Goldsmith: On Welcome Hill,
May 6, 1984, early-morning fog made the view from
Ann's living room look like a misty lake instead of
rolling hills. I hated to leave, remembering the wonderful preceding day, a tiring day, but one filled with the
joy of affirmation and amazed satisfaction. Four of
us had conceived an idea seven years ago to build a
studio for women artists and the same four women
had just spent a day reading the text of a book that
would tell the story. There had been too much to do —
photographing, arguing, deciding details — but at Ann's
there is always time to laugh, to tease, to remember.
The book is going to reflect all the best, I mused, as
I drove down the hairpin turns of Ann's drive. And

so it should. That building is gorgeous, and we did it. We realized an elaborate fantasy.

Since my last entry in the building logbook appears half way through, I wondered if the reader was going to be curious as to why a voice so present in the first part of the story was absent in the second half. Why the silence? They all, Ann S., Pat, Dolores, said, "Write something additional," and I said, "Sure," without a clue as to how to say something appropriate.

I was into the mist now, knowing that at this very moment it was still clear and lovely at the Studio. Being there with the building finished is so different. The cut in the woods, fondly called Matterbreast Blvd., looks as if it has always been there. The path from the Studio to the Guest House is wide now. The building has settled so nicely into its space. Because I had nothing to do with the finishing, it has a slightly unreal quality for me.

I had left the project feeling beaten and broken beyond what was fair with a back injury that caused months of immobility. The Studio vanished from my consciousness then, for if I thought of it I could only feel bitter and overcome with self-pity. I desperately concentrated on trying to get better and, eventually, came out on the other side of the hardest time of my life.

The drive from Welcome Hill to my home near Boston is familiar, like roots. I had made the trip so many times those many years ago I almost could drive it unconsciously. I had figured out lots of things along that route and worked out tensions. It is interesting

that the tensions surrounding the building of the Studio
are hardly mentioned in the text we read over line by
line. That figures. The log is a record of the building,
happy thoughts about progress and funny stories. We
wrote when we felt good, or moved, or poetic. No
one wanted to write the hard stuff. We worked that
out elsewhere, or we didn't. Some of us worked it out
physically, and badly. My back didn't go out just
because of the Studio, Goddess knows, but surely not
dealing directly with my feelings added to the spinal
weakness. I know that now. Some of us learned more
than how to pound nails and measure boards.

Noticing a section of the road that used to be
bumpy, now repaved, I return to the fond remembering
we four did this weekend. What a thrill it had been
when the first of the posts and beams went up — and
then, the added excitement when they were all in place
and the roof rafters could be bolted together at the
peak. I felt alive then, and able to live in the now.
Each day had its tasks, its set of accomplishments.
Progress might be slow sometimes, but still very see-
able. The touch of many women is in evidence. Further-
more, the Studio keeps changing as women live in it.
It is rearranged to meet the individual needs of each
woman artist, and improvements continue to happen.
The basic structure remains constant, with its lines and
angles and changing light patterns of the day and of
the season. Tranquility surrounds one in that space.

I will make this trip many more times, I am sure.
My soul needs to go to Welcome Hill from time to
time. Lasting friendships have been made and kept

there. Someday, I hope to be a resident, seeing the turn of each season and feeling the space anew. I wonder if the Goddess knows how very proud I am to have participated in the building of that special women's space.

Cr: A.R.S.

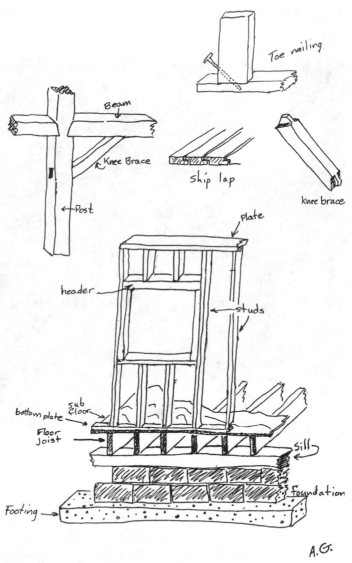

Toe nailing.

Beam

Knee Brace

Post

ship lap

knee brace

Plate

header

studs

sub floor

bottom plate

Floor Joist

sill

Foundation

Footing

A.G.

Glossary

Backhoe: a tractor-like piece of equipment that digs trenches real fast.

Battens: the vertical narrow boards that cover the seams between two wider vertical boards. A type of siding is called board and batten.

Building braces: boards placed triangularly to temporarily stabilize walls.

Circular saw: a hand-held power saw with a circular rotary blade, for making straight cuts.

Deck footings: footings (see below) that support a deck.

Footing: the cement base of the foundation, which sits on a ledge or below the frost line.

Framing: the structure of the walls.

Headers: horizontal pieces of lumber, 2 × 4s or 2 × 6s,
    marking the tops of doors or window openings.
Joists: horizontal timbers placed on edge to serve
    as a base for the floor. Usually they are 2 × 8s or
    2 × 10s.
Knee braces: diagonal pieces of wood that support
    the beams to keep the building square.
Lag bolts: bolts with screw threads rather than nuts.
Milled lumber: boards that are planed at the lumber
    mill and therefore smooth.
Plates: horizontal pieces of board at the top and bot-
    tom of a wall.
Pole saw: a pole with a saw at the end to prune
    branches too high to reach with a regular pruning
    saw.
Post: vertical structural timber of a post-and-beam
    construction (see below).
Post-and-beam: a type of building construction using
    heavy timbers as the frame of the structure.
Roof decking: the plywood on top of the roof rafters.
Saber saw: a power saw with a small blade that moves
    up and down; used for making curved cuts.
Sanitary land fill: the area around the foundation
    where the backhoe leaves a bit of a trench. It needs
    to be filled in and, in our case, got filled in with
    beer cans, clean trash, and mementoes, before it was
    covered with earth and flowers.
Sheetrock: fibrous wallboard that is made of plaster
    covered with heavy building paper.
Ship-lap walls: wallboards that overlap for a tight seal.

Siding: the outer skin of the house. In our case, it was
   board and batten.

Sills: the pieces of horizontal timber the whole house is
   built upon.

Sill plates: horizontal boards on which to place the
   studs (see below).

Studs: the vertical 2 × 4s or 2 × 6s that make up the
   skeletal structure of the walls.

Toenailing: nailing boards together by inserting nails
   at a 45 degree angle.

Wedging: a technique for forcing together boards laid
   side by side, as are flooring boards and siding.
   Often, warped boards require serious wedging.

A few of the publications of
THE NAIAD PRESS, INC.
P.O. Box 10543 • Tallahassee, Florida 32302
Mail orders welcome. Please include 15% postage.

Lesbian Nuns: Breaking Silence edited by Rosemary Curb and
Nancy Manahan. Autobiographies. 432 pp.
ISBN 0-930044-62-2 $9.95
ISBN 0-930044-63-0 $16.95

The Swashbuckler by Lee Lynch. A novel. 288 pp.
ISBN 0-930044-66-5 $7.95

Misfortune's Friend by Sarah Aldridge. A novel. 320 pp.
ISBN 0-930044-67-3 $7.95

A Studio of One's Own by Ann Stokes. Edited by Dolores
Klaich. Autobiography. 128 pp. ISBN 0-930044-64-9 $7.95

Sex Variant Women in Literature by Jeannette Howard Foster.
Literary history. 448 pp. ISBN 0-930044-65-7 $8.95

A Hot-Eyed Moderate by Jane Rule. Essays. 252 pp.
ISBN 0-930044-57-6 $7.95
ISBN 0-930044-59-2 $13.95

Inland Passage and Other Stories by Jane Rule. 288 pp.
ISBN 0-930044-56-8 $7.95
ISBN 0-930044-58-4 $13.95

We Too Are Drifting by Gale Wilhelm. A novel. 128 pp.
ISBN 0-930044-61-4 $6.95

Amateur City by Katherine V. Forrest. A mystery novel. 224 pp.
ISBN 0-930044-55-X $7.95

The Sophie Horowitz Story by Sarah Schulman. A novel. 176 pp.
ISBN 0-930044-54-1 $7.95

The Young in One Another's Arms by Jane Rule. A novel.
224 pp. ISBN 0-930044-53-3 $7.95

The Burnton Widows by Vicki P. McConnell. A mystery novel.
272 pp. ISBN 0-930044-52-5 $7.95

Old Dyke Tales by Lee Lynch. Short stories. 224 pp.
ISBN 0-930044-51-7 $7.95

Daughters of a Coral Dawn by Katherine V. Forrest. Science
fiction. 240 pp. ISBN 0-930044-50-9 $7.95

The Price of Salt by Claire Morgan. A novel. 288 pp.
ISBN 0-930044-49-5 $7.95

Against the Season by Jane Rule. A novel. 224 pp.
ISBN 0-930044-48-7 $7.95

Lovers in the Present Afternoon by Kathleen Fleming. A novel.
288 pp. ISBN 0-930044-46-0 $8.50

Toothpick House by Lee Lynch. A novel. 264 pp.
ISBN 0-930044-45-2 $7.95

Madame Aurora by Sarah Aldridge. A novel. 256 pp.
ISBN 0-930044-44-4 $7.95

Curious Wine by Katherine V. Forrest. A novel. 176 pp.
ISBN 0-930044-43-6 $7.50

Black Lesbian in White America by Anita Cornwell. Short stories,
essays, autobiography. 144 pp. ISBN 0-930044-41-X $7.50

Contract with the World by Jane Rule. A novel. 340 pp.
ISBN 0-930044-28-2 $7.95

Yantras of Womanlove by Tee A. Corinne. Photographs.
64 pp. ISBN 0-930044-30-4 $6.95

Mrs. Porter's Letter by Vicki P. McConnell. A mystery novel.
224 pp. ISBN 0-930044-29-0 $6.95

To the Cleveland Station by Carol Anne Douglas. A novel.
192 pp. ISBN 0-930044-27-4 $6.95

The Nesting Place by Sarah Aldridge. A novel. 224 pp.
ISBN 0-930044-26-6 $6.95

This Is Not for You by Jane Rule. A novel. 284 pp.
ISBN 0-930044-25-8 $7.95

Faultline by Sheila Ortiz Taylor. A novel. 140 pp.
ISBN 0-930044-24-X $6.95

The Lesbian in Literature by Barbara Grier. 3d ed. Foreword by
Maida Tilchen. A comprehensive bibliography. 240 pp.
ISBN 0-930044-23-1 $7.95

Anna's Country by Elizabeth Lang. A novel. 208 pp.
ISBN 0-930044-19-3 $6.95

Prism by Valerie Taylor. A novel. 158 pp.
ISBN 0-930044-18-5 $6.95

Black Lesbians: An Annotated Bibliography compiled by
J. R. Roberts. Foreword by Barbara Smith. 112 pp.
ISBN 0-930044-21-5 $5.95

The Marquise and the Novice by Victoria Ramstetter. A novel.
108 pp. ISBN 0-930044-16-9 $4.95

Labiaflowers by Tee A. Corinne. 40 pp.
ISBN 0-930044-20-7 $3.95

Outlander by Jane Rule. Short stories, essays. 207 pp.
ISBN 0-930044-17-7 $6.95

Sapphistry: The Book of Lesbian Sexuality by Pat Califia. 2nd
edition, revised. 195 pp. ISBN 0-930044-47-9 $7.95

All True Lovers by Sarah Aldridge. A novel. 292 pp.
ISBN 0-930044-10-X $6.95

A Woman Appeared to Me by Renee Vivien. Translated by
Jeannette H. Foster. A novel. xxxi, 65 pp.
ISBN 0-930044-06-1 $5.00

Cytherea's Breath by Sarah Aldridge. A novel. 240 pp.
ISBN 0-930044-02-9 $6.95

Tottie by Sarah Aldridge. A novel. 181 pp.
ISBN 0-930044-01-0 $6.95

The Latecomer by Sarah Aldridge. A novel. 107 pp.
ISBN 0-930044-00-2 $5.00

VOLUTE BOOKS

Journey to Fulfillment	by Valerie Taylor	$3.95
A World without Men	by Valerie Taylor	$3.95
Return to Lesbos	by Valerie Taylor	$3.95
Desert of the Heart	by Jane Rule	$3.95
Odd Girl Out	by Ann Bannon	$3.95
I Am a Woman	by Ann Bannon	$3.95
Women in the Shadows	by Ann Bannon	$3.95
Journey to a Woman	by Ann Bannon	$3.95
Beebo Brinker	by Ann Bannon	$3.95

These are just a few of the many Naiad Press titles. Please request a
complete catalog! We encourage and welcome direct mail orders from
individuals who have limited access to bookstores carrying our publications.